SECRET TO CREATING AN ABUNDANCE WEALTH

How to Build A Generational Wealth That Last

Stanley F. John

Copyright © 2022 Stanley F. John

All Right Reserved

Cover Designed By: Tammy Mike

Edited By: Julia Seth

The Scanning, uploading and distribution of this book without permission is a theft of the author's intellectual property if you would like permission to use material from the book (other than for review purposes).

Thank you for your support of the author's rights.

Table of Contents

Table of Contents 3
Introduction 4
   How to Make Your Life Bigger 9
Part Two 14
   Forge Your Way to Wealth 14
Part Two 22
   Your habits determine your level of wealth 22
   Recap 28
Part Three 30
   Mindset of Abundance 30
Part Five 42
   Long-Lasting Wealth 42

Introduction

The wealth of Nature and the deprivation that many people experience in their daily lives shouldn't be at odds with one another. You are in that gap when you claim that you don't have enough time or that there is never enough money since there is no disputing that time is unlimited and that riches may be eternally produced. Why don't you take a portion of it?

Anxiety over a loss of money has taken the place of a feeling of richness and contentment, particularly now that the economy has made financial shortage accessible to those who can least afford it. Lack of funds or time should not be a reason to give up. What about a lack of affection, lack of innovative ideas, or lack of emotional fulfillment?

At least, in theory, plenty should be universal. Even when you look around and realize that some individuals are considered luckier than others, bringing wealth into your own life should be more than a game of chance.

Let's go on with the idea that you can create anything you desire, which is the same as saying you can generate your luck. This presumption is preferable to depending on luck's ups and downs. If you wait for wonderful things to happen to you, you will already be defeated since negative things will inevitably come your way in life as well. You may, so to speak, alter the game in your favor rather than waiting passively to see whether you've won the lottery of life;

1. Transform adversity into opportunity

Pick one item that makes you feel bad today. Take one constructive step to lessen the negative before the day is through. Among them are the following:

Fix what can be mended, ask for assistance, seek wise counsel, walk away from things that can't be addressed, stand up for yourself, speak your truth, reduce tension, and consider your part in creating the problematic situation

There are many options. Any action, no matter how minor, starts to alter the feedback you are receiving.

2. Adopt a Balanced External Perspective

People tend to close up and retreat internally when things are terrible. "It's my issue" causes isolation, which exacerbates the feeling of lack and loss. Although I am aware that nobody wants to be a burden on others and that everyone wants to maintain their dignity, you should know that others have been in your position. They have dealt with scarcity and loss, endured suffering, and ultimately succeeded. Being in contact with a confidante who has done the thing is quite helpful.

3. Refrain from engaging in excessive futility

"I am powerless; there is no hope. Everybody hears these words: "Nothing will ever change or become better. The voice of futility endures because we were all once helpless and despairing children.

The voice of futility will drag you down to its level if you listen to it. So, resist the urge to adopt a pessimistic attitude. "This negative voice is not me," tell yourself. Reject the voice of futility gently but firmly, and if anything, positive occurs, no matter how tiny, remind yourself that the voice was incorrect.

4. Widen Your Perspective

Contraction is the worst adversary of plenty. These symptoms of contraction—in mind, body, and spirit—including feeling trapped, having trouble coming up with fresh ideas, feeling as if there is no way out, and carrying a heavy load.

The best buddy of plenty is expansion. It ushers in light, creating fresh opportunities. Your consciousness can see further and life is less constrained when you are calm and open.

How can you broaden your perspective?

Set aside sometime each day for solitude to start. The brain has a built-in system for resetting and restoring equilibrium. Give this system a go. Being pressed for time, putting up with stress and noise, and never taking a break to unwind are ineffective behaviors. At least twice a day, find a quiet area and spend a few minutes sitting there with your eyes closed. Allow yourself to find your core once again and meditate.

Following this instant solace, consider the following long-term actions. Your whole existence genuinely expands as a result of increasing your awareness:

How to Make Your Life Bigger

- Be enthusiastic about the experiences you add to your life.
- Be as receptive to suggestions as you can.
- Avoid using judgment, inflexible views, and prejudice to stop the feedback loop.
- Don't use denial to filter incoming data.
- Analyze opposing viewpoints as though they were your own.
- Take control of every aspect of your life.
- Being independent.
- Address psychological barriers like guilt and shame, which distort your perception of the world.
- Release your emotions; the greatest safeguard against being inflexible is emotional resilience.
- Do not keep secrets since they cause psychological darkness.
- Be open to changing who you are every day.

- Let go of the past and the future without regret.

Both cause suffering by harboring self-doubt.

To help you remember that your ultimate objective is growth, not a contraction, print off this list and consult it about once a month.

5. Accept Complete Responsibility

Here is a radical solution for victimization if you want it. Victims are ruled by outside forces—other people, events, or strokes of luck—and because these factors are uncontrollable, it seems only reasonable to abdicate responsibility for the negative aspects of your life.

It's like a poison seed that keeps sprouting up: "I can't help it." Recognizing that circumstances only change once a person stops seeking outside of themselves and begins to take responsibility is the answer. That's not the same as accepting responsibility.

You are expressing something constructive in its place:

- This is my life. Once you accept responsibility, you recover control over your life.
- You are also conveying a straightforward, unavoidable reality at the same time.

Who else might your life belong to if it isn't your own?

Nobody else has the resources—time, cash, effort, love—to offer you everything. Abundance originates internally. When you accept responsibility, you take ownership of everything—the good and the terrible.

Fortunately, the majority of the evil has already occurred, while the good still lies ahead in uncharted territory. Being accountable equates to embarking on your own life's path.

6. Create a More Idealistic Vision for Your Life

Some individuals are wealthy yet miserable; you may know someone who fits that description. However, it is impossible to be happy and unhappy at the same time. Even if material wealth might be beneficial, it cannot provide happiness on its own. The realization of a vision is what leads to fulfillment. The degree of satisfaction increases with increased eyesight.

A vision acts as a catalyst for prosperity. It starts several unnoticed processes. There is no hidden information here. As you have seen, awareness grows upon itself. Practice makes perfect, so you improve at things. Positive reinforcement encourages more optimism to follow. I understand that the phrase "feedback loop" seems antiseptic, yet it describes all you hope for, want, and imagine. Focused criticism is the greatest type to get.

You shouldn't be eating a sandwich and sending a pal a text while learning to ride a bike. Your main goal is to ride the bike. Similar to this, the vision you have for your life draws the elements necessary for mastery while excluding unnecessary deterrents. Once you are conscious of your vision, the winnowing process takes care of itself naturally and at a deep level of awareness.

With these tips, I hope you may approach wealth in a more upbeat manner and see it as a natural way to live and see oneself.

Part Two

Forge Your Way to Wealth

It doesn't need talent, good fortune, or privileged connections. You don't have to go to pricey weekend financial seminars or pick up the most recent strategies and ploys promoted by cunning salespeople.

The secret is that there are no secrets, as John Bogle wryly put it. Nobody will get wealthy by selling you information on how to acquire riches since it is in the public domain and easy to comprehend.

It's so simple that it can be described in just two words:

1. Make more money than you spend and smartly invest the surplus.

2. Establish easy daily routines that help you accumulate money.

I understand that you may be a bit let down.

You were searching for something innovative, creative, and novel—the crucial component that has been holding you back and would lead to ground-breaking outcomes. Every marketer attempts to offer the legendary "*secret*."

I'll offer you something that sounds quite similar to what Grandma would have said instead. But pay attention to experience's wisdom. I've trained hundreds of individuals, from poor debtors to successful businesspeople, and the pattern is clear.

I'm not the only one singing this tune, though.

Benjamin Franklin taught these identical facts hundreds of years ago, and many authorities, including J. Paul Getty, have reaffirmed them ever since. It is timeless advice that has stood the test of time and will probably also be effective for you (if you just put it into practice).

In other words, these two phrases contain the crucial knowledge you need to be wealthy in this lifetime with the maximum likelihood of success.

Spend less than you make and invest the difference as the first step towards building wealth.

How to handle your own money such that you build assets is summed up in the first phrase.

It clarifies the value of producing positive cash flow so that you may invest to generate more positive cash flow.

Observe how it combines three disparate but related concepts to create a single concept:

Spending less while earning more

3. Make sensible investment decisions.

There are several ways to accomplish this goal, but they all adhere to two fundamental principles:

- You may quickly cut your expenditure by practicing different types of frugality.

- You can immediately improve your income by using numerous tactics, such as changing jobs, receiving a raise, or launching a company.

Simply put, you need to make sure that your revenue is greater than your outgoing costs so that you have saved for future development and income.

Although the dual goals of cutting costs and increasing income are not mutually incompatible, they do need completely distinct mentalities.

Living more modestly takes self-control and frugality. It is challenging to achieve since, for the majority of individuals, taking this road involves making sacrifices. If so, being frugal is a long and challenging route to riches since you will always have to choose between aspirations for financial independence and lifestyle preferences.

Others find joy in simplifying their lives and choosing to put their earned cash toward financial independence objectives rather than wasting it on frivolous purchases.

Extremely thrifty people sometimes save 70% of their salary and become financially independent in less than ten years, but it's not for everyone.

Increasing the income component of the equation is an additional option. The benefit of this strategy is that since your earning potential is theoretically boundless, there is no theoretical limit to how quickly your wealth may increase.

The "fast way" to riches, according to many wealth gurus, is on the income side of the equation; nevertheless, if you don't master the spending side of the equation, you still face a high chance of failing because you'll make the all-too-common error of letting spending increase as quickly as income.

The most successful money creators combine attention to both sides of the issue. By limiting consumption and increasing income, they can maximize savings.

It's the fastest, safest route to more money saved for investments.

Because all the information you want is freely accessible in the public domain, the third part of the equation, which is to invest properly, is similarly straightforward.

You are not required to attend investing seminars or acquire exceptional knowledge. There are two tested routes:

1. Paper Assets: Traditional buy-and-hold strategies use inexpensive index funds and proven asset allocation theories. You can get everything you need at Vanguard Funds.

2. Real estate: Direct ownership of a property with a solid income flow in your neighborhood.

In conclusion, being financially free is fairly easy.

1. Spend less than you earn and intelligently invest the surplus.

2. Continue this process until your investment income surpasses your outgoings. You are then completely financially independent and immensely affluent.

However, despite the goal's desirability and the straightforward road that must be taken to get there, only a small percentage of people will attain financial independence.

This page was left blank intentionally

Part Two

Your habits determine your level of wealth

Because they don't develop wealth-producing behaviors, very few individuals become wealthy.

As you already know, there is a straightforward and well-tested strategy for accumulating money. The only thing left to do is to act consistently enough to attain the objective. and there is where the issues are.

The method for doing this is as follows:

[(Small, Wise Decisions)] [(Consistency) [(Time)]] = Riches

The single largest wealth killer is procrastination. You intend to complete it eventually. You are aware of what has to be done, yet there are always other priorities. The vehicle has to be fixed, the kids need braces, and the kitchen needs to be renovated.

Where the rubber hits the road is in action. Knowing what to do is one thing, but doing it is quite another. Because of this, habits are very important.

Habits are the reason lottery winners fail while postal employees become millions.

It doesn't matter whether you read **The Millionaire Next Door** by Stanley and Danko or Benjamin Franklin's essays from 250 years ago.

They all say the same thing: Successful money managers are what set wealthy individuals apart from others. They are wise with money. They do not make the most money. They don't have the best minds. They lack any specialized training. Simply put, they simply have decent financial practices.

The science underlying how money accumulates to build into wealth is what explains why sound financial practices are crucial.

Massive consequences may be produced by little adjustments made over an extended period. It's a simple route to financial security and the well-known "secret" to accumulating riches.

Daily behaviors are crucial for this reason

• Being frugal daily allows you to accumulate significant wealth over time by saving little sums of money every day that build and compound over time. For evidence, use this Latte Factor calculator.

• Your income potential will grow incrementally each day if you make it a practice to increase your earning potential via training and education.

Massive wealth may be produced by making little adjustments over an extended period.

Both of these routines will result in a widening gap between your income and expenses, which will boost your wealth at an accelerated pace. It is not a complicated science. It only consists of everyday routines focused on accumulating riches.

The habit drives the behavior, which results in the outcome. Cause and effect are straightforward.

The most straightforward approach for you to go from knowing how to develop money utilizing the above formula to doing what is necessary to attain the objective is via habits.

You don't need to struggle against significant difficulties or intellectualize the procedure. You don't need to prepare before preparing. Instead, just make a lifestyle change today that will help you achieve your financial objectives. Here are some possible places to start:

1. Enroll in an automated savings plan.

2. Join your employer's 401(k) plan (if they offer it).

3. Make a tiny sum of your mortgage prepayment.

4. Identify and cut off an unneeded spend.

5. Reduce clutter by selling unnecessary items (RV, boat, jewelry, etc.).

6. Fix something rather than buy a replacement.

7. Create a specialized area of knowledge in your field that may fetch a better salary.

8. Begin studying asset allocation or real estate investing.

Choose one habit, and begin it right now. Choose another habit to repeat after the first one until it gets ingrained in your life. After that, continue till you can see your money increase.

Procrastination is the biggest hindrance to money accumulation. The quickest method to stop procrastinating and take instant action is to form new habits.

Habits break down the whole process of accumulating money into little chunks that everybody can understand. Wealth is the result of the accumulation of all these little acts over a lifetime.

Recap

Spend less than you earn and intelligently invest the difference to increase your money, according to a straightforward formula.

Adopting wealth-building habits is an equally straightforward technique for putting the formula into practice and getting results.

Another format of it is seen here: *[(Small, Wise Decisions)] [(Consistency) [(Time)]] = Riches*

There is just one thing left to decide: will you put in the necessary effort?

This page was left blank intentionally

Part Three

Mindset of Abundance

The mentality of abundance encourages gratitude and appreciation for everything that one has in life. A mentality of plenty is the conviction that there is enough of everything for everyone in the world.

Your capacity for plenty influences both your personal and professional success. When you adopt an abundant mentality, you experience clarity, self-assurance, and competence. When you have a scarcity mindset, you are afraid of the future and think that there is a finite amount of everything in the universe.

More creativity and pleasure may be attained by adopting an abundant attitude. Additionally, it fosters beneficial behaviors and encourages appreciation and thankfulness.

I'll outline seven strategies for cultivating an abundant mentality in this essay. Having an affluent mindset makes you more driven, joyful, and appreciative of what you have.

You feel more thankful, appreciative, and self-confident when you are feeling plentiful. When you have an abundant mindset, you concentrate on the endless possibilities for progress and improvement.

Abundant perspective

A person with an abundant mentality concentrates on endless possibilities in both life and business. Instead of concentrating on the unpleasant aspects of their lives, they choose to highlight the good ones.

A person with an abundant attitude is appreciative, joyful, and creative. People with an abundant perspective also benefit from deeper connections, more favorable possibilities, and life-changing events.

A person who has an abundance mindset is optimistic and always seeking new opportunities to learn, develop, and accomplish the things that are most important to them. A person who has an abundance mentality sees each event as a chance to develop and learn, and they think that there is plenty for everyone.

Generous Thinking

You become happier and more inquisitive when you make it a point to think abundantly. You may feel clear, confident, and thankful when there is plenty.

Focusing on what you already have and the chances before you are what abundant thinking entails. An attitude of plenty fosters confidence and gratitude. Feelings of affluence may also improve your relationships and goal-setting.

The mindset of abundant thinking enables you to create a broader goal and take everyday action to realize it. When you have a larger perspective, you are more driven and live proactively. This enables you to enjoy what you do while also helping you prepare for the future.

Scarcity vs plenty attitude

Anyone who has an abundance attitude thinks that everything is plenty. People who are in plenty have more time, are thankful, and have more possibilities.

A person with a scarcity mindset has a zero-sum perspective. You feel that there are a limited amount of time, money, energy, and resources when you think in terms of scarcity. Either a scarcity mentality or an abundant mindset may be developed.

You may be prevented from accomplishing your objectives by a scarcity mentality. A person who has a scarcity mindset thinks there isn't enough for everyone. They think that everything needed to build a prosperous future is in short supply.

You could experience jealousy, guilt, and rage when you have a scarcity mentality. You could experience feelings of paralysis, depression, and overwhelm if you have a scarcity perspective.

A mentality of plenty helps you feel joyful, ecstatic, driven and prepared to take action.

How can one cultivate an attitude of abundance?

You can grow without boundaries or limits if you adopt an abundant mindset. You can also see possibilities everywhere, be clearer about your mission, and maintain thankfulness no matter what.

• Encourage exponential development as opposed to linear growth.

• Experience an abundance of creativity and inspiration

• Produce life-changing and unforgettable moments

How to cultivate an abundant mentality in 7 steps

To cultivate an abundant mentality, follow these 7 steps.

1. To live abundantly, put your attention on thankfulness.

A person who views life as abundant expresses thankfulness. They are content with what they have and do not harbor any envy toward others.

People with an abundant perspective don't feel bad about what they have or what others don't. They put more emphasis on appreciating who they are and what they have instead.

A mindset of abundance encourages people to deepen their appreciation and concentrate on their abilities. Additionally, they show gratitude for the individuals in their lives.

People with plenty develop the habit of finding the good in every circumstance. Instead of concentrating on what went wrong, they search for opportunities to learn.

2. Surround yourself with others who think in terms of plenty

A person who has an abundant attitude surrounds themselves with like-minded others. They look for devoted, sensible individuals. Additionally, they search for those who find the good in every situation.

People in plenty seek others who will encourage and push them onward. They seek others who will keep them responsible and recognize their accomplishments. A person with an abundant mindset seeks out those who can improve their way of thinking.

3. Live a prosperous life

It's crucial to have a picture of your ideal future self if you wish to live abundantly. Setting goals offers your life direction and a purpose while boosting your confidence. Setting goals boosts motivation and creates enthusiasm for the future.

Feelings of plenty are increased by having a clear vision. Additionally, it eliminates intricacy and complexity, which makes things seem easier. When you're feeling prosperous, your vision serves as a map. Additionally, it gives you the self-assurance and capacity to realize that goal.

Make a rich life with my goal-setting advice.

4. Concentrate on your distinctive skills

Focusing on your abilities is a sign of having an abundant attitude. Instead of attempting to strengthen your flaws, concentrate on your strongest suit.

You are aware of the effects that your words and deeds have on other people. It makes you feel as if there is enough. Additionally, it gives you the impression that you are making progress in the areas of your life that are most important to you.

Everything seems feasible when there is plenty. Feelings of affluence give you greater vitality, inventiveness, and self-assurance. A person with an abundant attitude constantly makes progress. They are aware that their advantages provide them with a chance to advance more quickly.

5. Continue to pursue your passions.

An individual who has an abundance mindset spends their time doing what they enjoy. This equips them to seize more significant possibilities.

Many individuals are aware that the quickest path to greater pleasure is to pursue their passions. Instead of engaging in activities they dislike, they concentrate on possibilities.

People with an abundance mindset concentrate on success and advancement. By participating in more of the things they love to do, they feel better about themselves.

Affluent individuals plan their days so that they may do more of the things they love to do. They decide what are the day's top priorities. They also devote the majority of their time to improving them.

They also honor their successes to increase sentiments of prosperity and advancement.

6. Develop an attitude of plenty.

The mindset of abundance thinking fosters optimism and self-assurance. Someone with a lot of thinking wants to learn and develop. To enhance their thinking and effectiveness, they seek out fresh information and insight.

Many individuals concentrate on strengthening their optimistic outlook. They look for persons who can advance them. To accomplish more and achieve more, they also take care of their bodies and minds.

The value of rest and exercise is understood by someone with an abundant mindset. They take care to eat well and schedule time for relaxation and renewal.

7. Increase plenty and banish scarcity

A person with an abundant mentality concentrates on increasing abundance. They pledge to do away with scarcity as well. They are aware of what fosters an abundant attitude and what fosters a scarcity mindset.

Abundant people are self-aware and motivated to advance themselves. They are on the hunt for anything that increases sensations of affluence. Additionally, they invest more effort in forming virtuous behaviors.

They also eliminate everything that promotes a scarcity mentality. People who believe in plenty benefit from feeling happier and more driven. As a result, they have more memorable experiences and feel more optimistic about the future.

Part Five

Long-Lasting Wealth

Each of Warren Buffet's children received a $2 billion foundation gift. When Gloria Vanderbilt was just 15 months old, she inherited a trust fund worth $36 million. There are several well-known tales of one generation leaving the next significant wealth.

The ordinary individual saves as much as they can while they can in the hopes of leaving something behind, such as an inheritance that would serve as a down payment for a first house or college costs that would help a young person start with less debt.

Learning how to create generational wealth, in whatever form that may take for you, is important if you want to leave a lasting legacy.

These actions are helpful.

Establish your financial legacy.

Consider these three figures:

• The median inheritance is $55,000.

• Parents cover little under half of their children's college expenses.

Almost half of all parents provided financial support to their adult children throughout the epidemic. Leaving money behind after your death, funding a college education, and offering support during hard times are a few instances of how individuals leave money behind. They serve as illustrations of how each financial inheritance differs from the others in appearance and timing.

We all tend to think of a legacy as 'passing assets,' but it's more complicated than that, according to Stanley Poorman, a financial advisor with

Principal. "What if your family experiences became your legacy? Finding a way to utilize your money now to leave a living legacy then becomes the problem.

According to Heather Winston, associate director of financial counseling and planning at Principal, the first step could simply be to determine what you're going to leave the next generation before having a conversation about it.

The discussion need not be just financial, she believes. "Perhaps it's about providing financial support for future generations while you're still living or leaving a material legacy like a home or automobile once you are away.

Discuss that legacy with the next generation.

You may have been lucky enough to pay off all of your debt throughout your lifetime, take your family on holidays, and pay for a part of your child's tuition.

According to Poorman, *"If you're the first generation that's been able to generate money, you're exhibiting your beliefs and imparting them to others."*

Maybe you've also decided to donate money to a charity. Be honest with your loved ones about your desires so they can support them when you pass away and understand your choices.

Winston claims that *we act as if our life is endless when, regrettably, it isn't.* The 'why' behind your wishes should be communicated during these conversations, which should be had early on and frequently.

Include the objectives for your financial legacy in your yearly spending plan and long-term financial strategy. Say you want to set aside money in the next year or two for a new kitchen remodel. Most likely, you've already considered how much it might cost and how you might save money for the project.

Use the same strategy to create wealth for future generations. Setting up and contributing to an education savings plan will assist if your objective is to pay for a year of college. Making a rough budget and setting up an automatic savings deposit for vacations only will help you get closer to your goal of giving a paid annual family vacation.

In the end, Winston argues, "it's not only thinking about it but doing it, and that may be hard." But that's what separates fantasy from reality. You must give it physical form for it to be genuine.

Complete paperwork to safeguard your legacy.

Examine the items you should include in your estate plan if you do wish to leave anything to others.

A will is the most fundamental estate planning instrument. Many individuals decide to include a trust in their estate plan since it may sometimes be challenging to leave your possessions to others via a will. This legal framework spells out what happens to your property and who is in charge of carrying out your intentions.

Together with your legal counsel, complete these forms, and after that speak with a financial expert at least once a year to track your progress toward your objectives.

Consider accumulating money for future generations gradually.

While still in high school, Warren Buffet delivered newspapers and worked at his grandfather's grocery shop. He still resides in the Omaha,

Nebraska, home he purchased in 1957. Winston claims that Buffet made extremely intentional choices to build a fortune and instruct future generations of investors.

Nobody here is Buffet. But suppose one of your financial legacy objectives was to cover your children's whole college expenses. Perhaps you can only save enough money to cover half of the tuition and fees. Even if you may feel like you fell short of your objective, think about this: There is a chance that your children's education may bring riches down to you. The lifetime earnings of college graduates are at least $630,000 more than those with just a high school education.

It justifies the effort.

Winston explains, "It all boils down to the idea that money is only a tool. It does not take the place of the value that a person offers. That's a wise last observation regarding accumulating wealth: It's often gradual from one generation to the next.

According to Winston, *"each generation can and usually does a bit more."* "You may leave your heirs your thoughts and ideas about what you want, why you want it, and how you hope their lives will be. But it will be up to them to decide how to interpret it.

www.ingramcontent.com/pod-product-compliance
Lightning Source LLC
Chambersburg PA
CBHW050315220526
45465CB00005B/1994